COPYRIGHT DISCLAIMER UNDER SECTION 107 OF THE COPYRIGHT ACT 1976

Copyright Disclaimer Under Section 107 of the Copyright Act 1976, allowance is made for "fair use" for purposes such as criticism, comment, news reporting, teaching, scholarship, and research. Fair use is a use permitted by copyright statute that might otherwise be infringing. Non-profit, educational or personal use tips the balance in favor of fair use.

All material appearing in *21 Orbits* is protected by copyright under U.S. Copyright laws and is the property of Kennedy Williams. You may not copy, reproduce, distribute, publish, display, perform, modify, create derivative works, transmit, or in any way exploit any such content, nor may you distribute any part of this content over any network, including a local area network, sell or offer it for sale, or use such content to construct any kind of database. You may not alter or remove any copyright or other notice from copies of the content in *21 Orbits*. Copying or storing any content except as provided above is expressly prohibited without prior written permission of the copyright holder.

All rights reserved.

21 Orbits

by Kennedy Williams

"...and when my time is up, have I done enough?"

-Lin-Manuel Miranda

Table of Contents

"U Up?- A Modern Love Story   ...p 7

Gingerbread & Morphine- A   ...p 19
         Reflection

Year of the Groundhog   ...p 33

Breakup Party   ...p 38

The Countdown   ...p 50

"U Up?"- A Modern Love Story

12:48AM

    Lust. Intimacy. Three fragile words that slither from a snake's mouth. *I love u* texted Mr. Anonymous. *But, god, how I'd love to see* more *of u*. Mr. Anonymous, the man sending me texts from behind a screen, and Whatshisname from my past are two different people- both brought together through their selfishness and destruction. Mr. Anonymous- an unknown man digging himself into a hole in my Instagram messages. Whatshisname- a boy from my elementary school days of whom I once believed I would marry. Even now, they merge together in my mind, like two candle wicks slowly burning into one bitter, gray ash. That's the thing with men; there's a time span in their early twenties in which the sight of adolescent breasts is all that they crave. It must start in high school when the seniors hunt down freshman girls, trick them and corner them in their cave, bite their flesh, and then abandon them at their weakest point. Broken wings can be repaired, but a soul- animal or human- is a delicate, god-like creature that must be handled with care. But lust is an obsession, and obsessions are uncontrollable. They stem from the most animalistic part of the psyche, triggered by microscopic chemicals in the brain. Even the satiation of obtaining something cannot last forever, though, which results in the inevitable cycle of hunger and desperation. Men justify. Men falsify. Men kill portions of themselves that they envy in women.

And most importantly, men waste what little time the universe has offered them in attempt to locate what it reserved for herself.

Women, goddesses of all things delicate, possess magic that men lack, and men presume that little girls can offer a taste of it. Afterall, women are intelligent creatures; they have learned to lock away the most sensitive parts of the body and mind or, in many cases, disguise/hide it from the public eye. Teenage girls are much easier. They are trusting, persuadable, impressionable, gullible, and easily intimidated. They will slide their blouse to the side, tease boys with the slightest bit of glowing skin, and kiss with a passion that tastes like cherry lip balm because they have a desperate need to feel loved. At least that's what I envision myself doing as I, in reality, lay under my comforter with one leg sprawled out in the summer air. Thoughts of where I fall on the male's version of a femininity scale keep me up at night, but alas, my alarm clock is too bright for me to sleep anyways.

12:52AM

It's astonishing that, even after the most heinous act committed against me, I cannot remember my offender's name. Maybe the memory is blurred from it happening so long ago, as I was merely a twelve-year-old. Perhaps it was actually insignificant and should not bother me as much as it did. Or maybe I intentionally forgot it, as he is not deserving of a place in my subconscious. Whatshisname has probably changed, grown into a man of authority and respect. I know he has found a woman of pure beauty, and I know that she knows everything. She's always been good at social manipulation. The public is only allowed to see what she portrays, and that's exactly how the secret has been kept for so long. He probably laces her neck in the finest pearls, to which she ignores all of his wrongdoings, and he kisses the crevices of her collarbones. I hope that just as his lips make contact with her skin, Whatshisname is haunted by flashbacks of his crime in which I was forced to be an accomplice. He deserves to be happy, as every human does, but he should also have to experience the same gut-trembling sensation that creeps up at the most intimate of times.

1:08AM

U still there? I was guilty of double texting, too, but never in moments of such delicacy. There's always the lingering possibility that the anonymous man had no intention of degrading my sense of self, but each plea dug deeper into my skin and threatened to make me bleed out every day in class. Would the blood pool around my feet? Would it stain the Converse my mother got me for my sixteenth birthday? Would the school janitor have to re-mop his freshly waxed floor? Were my classmates criticizing the notifications abruptly interrupting every lecture, or were they blissfully unaware? Maybe everyone's always known, or rather assumed, who I am- secretive, lustful, revealing, a tease. It all started so young, as I was freshly hatched and had taken a mere two steps from the nest when I learned to chirp a mating song. Whatshisname surely told everyone about the way my feathers looked beneath the hand-me-down jeans; the way the male teachers looked at me some days proved they, too, had imagined the curve of my back as I was pinned underneath them. They could never have as much fun with it, though, as they knew me personally. And what is the excitement in kissing one's lips when they have already spoken too much about themselves? Innocence and avoidance are the driving factors here. It's what makes men want you. They can't control themselves when they have full control of you. *C'mon. Be a good girl. I know ur awake i can see ur active.*

1:22AM

Whatshisname? What is his fucking name? It shouldn't matter, but god it does. He and my ex-best friend have been seeing each other the past few years, despite her knowledge of what he did, and it never fails to make my skin crawl. She was the first person to know the length of him, what cologne he wore and how it suffocated me, the exact video game that he beat me in, the way Wendy's curly fries lingered on his breath, and how my first kiss was tainted by his tongue that nearly choked me out. She knew every erotic detail, down to the sound his belt buckle made when it hit the floor. Only the universe knows how many times Whatshisname asked me to go down on him, as it was too many for me to count, and how small he made me feel for neglecting to hold up my end of the deal. "You lost the game." "What do you want? To be kissed? I'll give you that if you just do it." "Come on. Don't be a fucking tease. You promised." "I don't have to finish. Please." He whimpered while twiddling his thumbs, looking like whipped puppy.

1:25AM

Astrology could partially be to blame. Some miraculous, randomized formation of the stars and planets could have tugged the both of us into an undeniable spiral of hormones. Had I tucked black tourmaline into the confines of my sports bra, the negative energy could have bounced away from me. Instead, I wore a rose quartz necklace and welcomed any form of love that was gravitating towards me. Whatshisname told me it was beautiful once, and so I wore it every day.

1:27AM

The man in my phone and Whatshisname have begun to intertwine too closely together in my thoughts. They both wanted to play a game with my mind, to make me solve a puzzle while they held the last piece behind their backs. I have spent hours of my adolescence searching for the piece, peering in my brassiere and flipping through pornography magazines. Nothing fit. My body didn't bend the way that models did, such elegant back arches with delicate hand placements, and I sure as hell didn't have the sexual attraction that the good guys wanted. But that piece has to exist somewhere. Would they still want me when I matured- when I had fuller breasts and an actual libido? That must have been the missing piece- maturity- and it makes sense that they would throw it away. Sarah, the dear ex-best friend, has never matured. With a five-foot tall stature, underdeveloped facial structures, and virgin hair that lacks heat damage, she is perfectly childlike. That has to be it. Whatshisname isn't capable of love; he is merely responsible for twisting the narrative, reassuring others that he simply likes short women: Yes, her cheeks blush from the slightest touch. Of course, her humor is that of a twelve-year-old's. Duh, she only listens to 5 Seconds of Summer and One Direction. Yeah, her victim mentality and controlling behavior is immature and disgusting. But he loves her for who she is, not because she is such a child! Damn you for thinking anything less than that. You need to sleep.

1:29AM

Ur mom won't find out right? Mom knew about the assault. She knew the week after it happened, actually. I don't remember how I told her, I just know it was nonchalant in an attempt to appear strong and unbothered. What twelve-year-old doesn't want to appear impenetrable to their parents? Instead of marching her ass to his house, dragging him out by the hair, and beating him with the nearest tree limb she could find, Mom shrugged it off. "You learned your lesson. Don't be going to boys' houses unsupervised. Hey, can you hand me that bag? I need to throw these away." Mom turned a corner, and we never spoke of it again.

1:31AM

I found a place we can hookup at near the railroad, kinda in the tree line. Nobody will know. U on birth control? Was my dad this vulgar when he was young? He's been married three other times, which could be due to his constant obsession with younger women. I'm a lot of things, but I am most certainly not stupid; the rumors were everywhere, uncanny evidence was sprawled throughout the house, and my parents' relationship was dwindling. From my perspective, my mother hasn't aged since the day she turned thirty, but her eyes have slightly dimmed. But my dad surely saw it differently. Having a third child, and considering that I was much younger than my half-sisters, had solidified the fact that she was no longer in her prime and resulted in few noticeable physical changes. My father began to discard her, as he did with his past wives at the first glimpse of a gray hair. Someone else had caught his eye anyways, and she resembled my mother in every way possible. Her name sounded like windchimes, her body radiated youth due to an eating disorder, and she always wore the brightest red lipstick. Cheerleading uniforms, pictures of her father, and Taylor Swift posters decorated her room, barely hiding the mural of Chicago that my mother had hand-painted on her wall. The girl my father chose over my mother was my very own half-sister. *If not I can get some Trojans. I have liquor to calm ur nerves too if u need it gorgeous.*

1:32AM

Whatshisname will be turning twenty-three soon. He'll be at some bar, Sarah by his side, as he orders pint after pint from a waitress in skimpy clothing. They'll be so carefree and in the moment. LED lights will make Sarah's skin glow. Red. Blue. Purple. Red. Blue. Purple. Which color will Whatshisname think her dewy skin looks best in? *Can't wait to see that necklace hanging from ur neck. It suits ur skin tone so well...* Dad just turned sixty-one. He's celebrating retirement by kayaking every lake in a fifty-mile radius, only stopping to request a sandwich from his girlfriend. He always tells the same story of how he used to work on the railroad before marrying my mom. *My hand would look better around it though...* Mr. Anonymous will be going into his mid-twenties. His Facebook is flooded with congratulations and celebratory posts. He just graduated college, and he cannot wait to begin his career as a children's pastor. Parents and former teachers praise him and request the date of which he will begin his teachings. *Helloooo?* I will be twenty-one next month. And I am disintegrating.

1:33AM

Hey u still haven't responded but i saw ur post on facebook. Hope ur okay and i'm sorry ur feeling so down. Not sure what's going on but just wanted to tell u that ur beautiful and i miss seeing u in the school hallways. Growing up sucks lol, enjoy ur youth while u can. Graduation comes and goes and next thing u know, ur 21 like me and don't even have time to tie ur shoes. So don't dwell on things so much. Stress only gets worse from here haha. Anyways. I went ahead and got the trojans so u don't have to worry about that. Also got some wine coolers bc i know how lightweight i was when i was ur age. I can pick u up tonight if ur down. Just don't tell anyone. My parents think I'm going out to eat with friends and my friends think i am with my parents. Don't wanna get caught in a lie.

1:34AM

Panic attacks never get easier. My therapist recommends that I count backwards from one hundred while focusing on breathing, but I somehow always get stuck after eighty-two. The hardest part of it all is the knowing. Knowledge is brutal. Each breath is just another memory flooding back, demonstrating even more examples as to why I should hyperventilate and disregard the truth of it all. I know in my heart of hearts that Whatshisname never wakes up in a sweat, whether he dreams of seeing himself in the reflection my necklace or not. I also know that my dad has probably outgrown his obsession with my sister and that she has never spoken a word of it. She and I haven't even had a conversation in nearly five years now, so there's no reason for my thoughts about it to exist. Mr. Anonymous is as well aware as I am that his secret is safe with me because I could never damage his career. He could take mine away if he wanted to retaliate, as the pictures of me reside in his phone are a looming threat above my head. At the end of the day, or in the middle of the night rather, it's just me and the stars. The universe has seen it all, every moment in history and each man's guilty pleasure, and my experience doesn't make a dent in human existence. For now, I will persuade myself that it is all irrelevant. The time on my clock is a façade made by men in order to wake before the roosters, and memories are nothing short of an electrical charge in my neurons. Nothing exists. Not obsession, not knowledge. Not bravery, not cowardice. Not quartz, not tourmaline. Not Whatshisname, not Anon.

3:15AM

Hey, sorry I haven't responded. Just been busy with school and stuff. I think we need to talk, I finally responded. It all had to end.

3:17AM

U up?

Gingerbread & Morphine- A Reflection

Death is subjective. According to the Oxford Dictionary, death is "the end of life; the permanent cessation of the vital functions of a person, animal, plant, or other organism". Yet if you ask a philosopher about their definition of death, you might receive a plethora of answers ranging from new beginnings, the formation of newfangled life, spiritual awakenings, or some muscular being with a sword that may not let you into the kingdom because you liked girls. Doctors and surgeons alike will say it's the lack of brain activity. Morticians will recognize that it's a paycheck, nothing more and nothing less. I do not know if any of these depictions are true; what I do know is that, when I was six years old, I had a major seizure and was resuscitated by my father. While what seemed like dozens of worried bodies gathered around my hospital bed, I opened my eyes and spoke two simple words to my mother- "I'm hungry."

You see, mortality can be completely meaningless, empty, unfulfilling, or even entirely unnoticed. But what happens when the inevitable ending interrupts an aspect of our lives without stealing a soul? Having this happen is worse than any eternal hell that one could be damned to. For example, you have dedicated years of your life to a specific craft, one that takes talent and dedication, only to find yourself turned away from those in a higher rank than you. It isn't the criticism, though that can play a part in it, but rather the feeling of your most vulnerable work being discarded like a piece of plastic in a landfill. How does one come back from that? How do you go from being a McDonald's wrapper thrown out of a teenager's Honda Civic to being an artist who lets every consumer into their minds? I don't know that there is an answer, but the trauma must at least leave a visible scar.

    There were other periods of my life in which I was on death's doorstep, including that of chronic tonsilitis that turned my tonsils black, pneumonia a few months after being diagnosed with childhood epilepsy, bronchitis with a 104-degree fever for a week solid, and having the flu for four years in a row all before the ripe age of seventeen. You eventually grow accustomed to feeling like a guinea pig in a laboratory though, at least when it begins at such an early age. Wires and sensors attached to my six-year-old skull was scary at first, but if you ask my mom about my reaction, she will tell the story of how I slept peacefully in an MRI machine around the same time period. It sounded like a thousand hammers were circling around my brain, but I didn't mind. I was accustomed. I was rewarded and praised. I was the talk of the town- the child on the top of every church's prayer list. Out of everything given to me at the time, I remember the stuffed lamb the most. Bedbound little me rolled over one afternoon to the delicately placed Webkinz plush. It was soft and warm, presumably from the fabric soaking up sunlight from the window it rested in front of. I cannot remember where or who it came from, but I do know that's when I realized I could milk the system. I would continue to play weak for the attention for a while. But when the Grim Reaper returned after my sixteenth birthday, I didn't want the God-like devotion. In fact, attention and sympathy were the last things I wanted. What I really desired was for someone to let me the hell out my hospital bed so that I could go to the gym or run a marathon. But alas, I was only given a scar across my stomach.

 My second encounter with death started off as a normal day, which is eerie in retrospect. Early sailors describe it best- the calm before the storm- but the thought of death approaching rapidly and out of nowhere is more than overwhelming when the only ship you have is your body. The stomach pain was minimal and dull, and I shrugged it off as menstrual cramps at first. I was forced to comfort myself with another reason when the nausea and fatigue set in, so I blamed what I despised most- food. My ex-boyfriend and I had baked gingerbread cookies a few hours prior to me laying in my bathroom in agony, so I convinced myself that I was experiencing some form of food poisoning.

 Ten tablespoons of unsalted butter. *1,020 calories.* 3/4 cup of brown sugar. *622 calories.* 2/3 cup of unsulphured molasses. *655 calories.* One large egg. *70 calories.* One teaspoon of pure vanilla extract. *12 calories.* 3 ½ cups of all-purpose flour.

1,593 calories. One teaspoon of baking soda. *0 calories.* Half a teaspoon of salt. *0 calories.* One tablespoon of ground ginger. *17 calories.* One tablespoon of ground cinnamon. *0.7 calories.* Half a teaspoon of ground allspice. *2 calories.* Half a teaspoon of ground cloves. *3 calories.* Optional: cookie icing. *660 calories. A whopping total of 4,594.7 calories. 4,594.7 calories divided among 24 servings is a yield of 193.95 calories per gingerbread cookie.* I ate half of one and promised myself I would resume my diet the following morning.

Evening crept by as I laid sprawled out on the living room couch. Exhaustion hit so hard and caused me to fall asleep where I was, but I awoke in the middle of the night in a panic. My immediate instinct was to dart into the bathroom and slow my heartrate. *Thump, thump. Thump, thump.* Stomach acid crept up my throat while I begged God to let me release the bile from my body. *Thump, thump. Thump, thump.* Praying was to no avail. I hadn't eaten a full meal, besides the gingerbread cookie, in well-over twenty-four hours at that point due to the slight discomfort in my abdomen all day, so there was nothing to release in the first place. Sweat dripped slowly from my hair follicles, caressing my brightly blushed cheeks before finally plopping onto the porcelain I was clinging to. *Thump, thump. Thump, thump.* Something was wrong. Really, really wrong.

Standing up, fumbling like a young doe, I tried to whip my hair into a bun. Then, and I have tried to research why exactly this happened, I blacked out and hit the ground. Something in my blood pressure must have changed, causing the sudden fainting spell that lasted for a few moments. I never found the exact cause, though. When I came to, I repeated the same motion as to avoid getting bile in my hair, lifting my arms and grasping at my hair. *Thump, thump. Thump, thump.* I hit the ground again. This time I soaked in the coolness of the tile while my mind wondered aimlessly. I questioned if Mom would find me there, curled into the fetal position and deceased from a mysterious illness. *Would she find out?* I thought. Even in my weakest moment, I didn't want my mom to know. She didn't deserve to discover that her youngest child had deprived herself of food for months. She obviously saw the rapid weight loss- forty pounds in less than three months- and the panic attacks when I couldn't work out. But I wanted her to remember me as a 5K champion. The girl who was at the top of her class and dating the football coach's son. The girl who survived so many battles- epilepsy, divorced parents, poverty, everything. Mostly, I wanted her to remember me as the child that wrote her heart out and had just won first in the state for it… only a month prior.

When I was younger, maybe eleven or so, I used to plead with my mother to let me stay at my grandma's house. She was always reluctant because of my health, but I assured her I would be okay, that I would be in good hands. Mom would sometimes cave in and let me go. Truthfully, I mainly wanted to see my cousin. Taylor and I played together on a regular basis, but Grandma's house was different. It was small, comforting, and right across from the park. The walls were caked in tobacco smoke, threatening to peel off at any given moment. Roasted foods simmered and begged us to eat them as we snacked on candies and sipped on whatever juice was in the fridge. Our Paw Paw would let us play in the old cars in the yard; they never worked but it was fun to pretend to be an adult, to be independent and free for a moment. One day specifically, Taylor and I decided to sneak into the kitchen when it was late enough that nobody would find us. "Just one. She'll never notice," Taylor said while stealing a cigarette. "I don't know," I replied apprehensively. Conversation, mostly arguing, flowed between us, to which I eventually felt pressured enough to take a hit. Dopamine instantly flowed through my veins and made my head spin. Smoke drifted in and out of my lungs, death teasing me from another dimension. Knowing it could kill us- that it would lead to others being in pain- was enthralling.

    At some point during the night of anguish, I regained enough strength to stumble into my mother's bedroom. Darkness surrounded me which felt nice after being in a bright, liminal space for what felt like forever. She shot up out of bed and must have been panicked, as I never interrupted her sleep. "Something's wrong," I spoke. What I thought was sweat trickled down my face again. I hadn't realized I was crying like a newborn until much later. She asked me what was wrong and from there, the conversation is a blur. Mom assumed I had a nasty stomach bug and sent me back to bed. I wouldn't wake up until 3PM the next day having missed school, phone calls, and worried texts. Mom found me on the couch, unable to form a proper sentence, and rushed me to our local doctor's office where they would break the news of my ungodly high fever. I was fed ibuprofen and sent in the lab to get an CT scan. One of the pretty nurses handed me a Styrofoam cup full of lemonade, or that's what she called it. "Drink all of this," she spoke sympathetically. Her hands lingered on mine for a few moments before she finally withdrew them. As I drank the lemonade, I cried again, heavier this time, and Mom rubbed my back.

  Vulnerability always made me feel like a child again- helpless and afraid. Drinking a concoction of barium sulfate and lemon flavoring while my insides felt like fiery sandpaper was **not** one of the highlights of being the "sick kid". The only thing worse than that was the injection they used before rolling me into the CT machine. The nurse warned, "You might feel warm, like you peed your pants." I laughed and said that it would be a cakewalk in comparison to the pain I was in. God himself spited me upon hearing that, as the injection burned every vein in my body. My blood felt like it was boiling as my body rejected it, and it was at that point of which I lost all memory. The rest of the night is hazy and somewhat lost in the depths of my memory. Mom drove us with the speed of a Mario Kart character to the hospital that the doctor had recommended, and the morphine I received felt like heaven on earth. Pain drifted away for the first time in nearly two days, to which I felt at ease and slipped into sleep. Very vaguely, I remember waking up after surgery and begging for water. I was spoon-fed ice chips from my mother, and my father stared at me in disbelief. I was disoriented from anesthesia and wondered why I hadn't died on the surgeon's table. Sleep all but consumed me after only two or three pieces of ice.

    I awoke in the hospital the next morning and was immediately bombarded with doctors and questions. My surgeon came in pulled my gown up, revealing every corner and crevice of the body I hated so much. Mom, Dad, my boyfriend, sister, and stepmom all saw everything. They saw the fresh wound that would soon scab over, the swelling, and the portions of me that I had never shown to anyone. Still completely out of it, I whimpered at the pressure of his hand on my abdomen. *I should have died.* He turned to my mother and gave her more worries than she came in with, putting into her mind that I would have died had we showed up thirty minutes later. *My stomach feels huge.* He also made himself the hero by making it known that he was the only one willing to come in so late to give me an appendectomy. *Why didn't I die?* More useless information was spouted as my mom sat out flowers that my sister Holly had sent. The vase was a beautiful blue, decorated with the most delicate yellow bird. *I need to get up, to walk. To run.* I fell back into an anxiety-ridden sleep.

    Everyone at school attempted to check in- phone calls, text messages, concerned emails from teachers. Posts were made on Facebook about how beautiful and successful I was. "Get well soon, Kennedy!" quoted people that I didn't know in the comment sections. I felt like I had come full circle again. I was a victim of a sudden, horrible illness and for some reason, everyone had something to say about it. Mom attempted to console them by saying I was okay, though it appeared that she was mainly trying to console herself. In between social media breaks and nurse visits, Mom would sneak in snacks that I liked. She brought Goldfish crackers, Pop-Tarts, and other comfort foods that I wasn't supposed to be consuming on my liquid diet. I nibbled here and there but was ultimately in too much discomfort. Thankfully, I was discharged the following morning and permitted to take as much time off as I needed. People were fine with it, as long as I came back healthy and creative/competitive as ever. That's all they saw. Creative, smart, brave, fragile, little Kennedy.

    Speaking of small things, I've always wondered what happened to that damned stuffed lamb. Perhaps it had found a new home after being dumped at Goodwill by my mother. Better yet, maybe it was in hiding in the attic of my childhood home, dusty and alone, watching the days tick by and longing for my story to conclude. Had I lost it at a park upon becoming infatuated with the swing set? Had another child found the lamb at the park, soaked by rain and speckled in dirt, and taken it home where it could be loved better than before? Where had the interest been lost in such a precious plushy? The answer is unknown, unlike the resolution to the tobacco fiasco. As for smoking cigarettes with Taylor, my mom had found out the day after it happened. We confessed everything to her even though she would have never had the slightest clue. Grandma's house was forever canceled from my schedule, and seeing Taylor became a rare treat. But as for that stupid, beloved Webkinz, I still don't know what happened. Endings, death specifically, is the biggest part of life. Relationships, friendships, jobs, experiences, movies, stories, everything- it all has a resolution. Cessation. But is there a true way to define it? How can one define death when each person views a truth differently? One may see the lamb as a temporary solution- a mere distraction- that was destined to fade into oblivion. Another one may see that the lamb was never alive and has been dead since the cotton was plucked and stuffed. And yet I don't know that the lamb's story will ever end, as it doesn't exist in my world anymore and is unable to be objectified in my version of truth.

  Panic ensued when I got home and saw my true self in the mirror. My once slim figure had turned back into what it had been four months prior. I was swollen, damaged, and insignificant again. Screams and sounds of heartache resonated through the house as I stepped on the bathroom scale. *Thump, thump. Thump, thump.* Ten pounds gained in two days. It happened so fast. *Thump, thump. Thump, thump.* My heart was threatening to beat out of my chest, and my palms were clammy and gripped tightly together. I needed to run. To escape. To never eat anything ever again. *Thump, thump. Thump, thump.* The pounding wasn't coming from my chest as I thought it was; it was my mom frantically trying to get me to unlock the bathroom door. Once more, she thought her baby was losing her life. Upon letting her in, her arms snaked around me out of sympathy. I was alive, if that's what one would call it. Alive, but not living. She would learn everything about me, everything that had completely consumed me for months on end, within a matter of moments. And at the very end of the most heart-wrenching conversation of my life, I told her, "I'm hungry." She smiled, remembering that dumb phrase.

    I wish I could say that everything immediately improved from there on out, but it would be nothing short of a lie, a deeply fabricated sentiment. Two trips to Los Angeles, one to New York City, and an event in Savannah, Georgia were all taken up by intrusive thoughts of anorexic whispers. Where I should have been indulging in the world's finest foods, I begged my sister to find a local gym where I could run. Recovery was a process of trial and error- relapse and breakdowns. To this day, I still have fear-foods, picky eating, and day-long relapses. There was no real "cure" to what I had been through, but I had realized something. I realized that death is subjective. Most people argue that there is no concept of personal death, but that is asinine and far from the truth. Every moment, every chapter of one's life is death to who you previously were. I should have died when my appendix failed. I should have died when I stopped breathing at only six years old. I should have died when I bottomed out on every nutrient in my body, when my iron was so low that they had to do an infusion. Yet, each time meant something different. Each experience was a varying, dramatic end to the old version of me. That is why death is subjective.

    Life is too short to worry about the perspective of other people. Whether one is worried about appearance, work ethic, skillset, career paths, school, personality, or anything in between, it is vital to remember how opinionated it all is. Learning that everyone's version of who I am is different, perhaps because of one insignificant moment in life's timeline, was the most valuable lesson from the many deaths I have had. After all, there are things much worse than actually passing away and leaving this planet, such as focusing on the things that one cannot change. Truth, and all life-altering events, differ upon who is asked, meaning that we must learn to focus on the things that revolve around life. Live as each moment is the last- the last bite, the last visit, the last goodbye.

Year of the Groundhog

"Don't fucking do it," I spat at my toothpaste tube, my chin pressed firmly against clasped palms. "For the love of God."

But it did it. Again. A small squelching sound- that damned nauseating, repulsive, repetitive, squish-of-paste sound. Something so typical, after five days of hearing it in the exact same way, had become too much. I glanced up at the mirror and let out a blood-curdling scream, chunking the Colgate at the wall and punching the face that stared back at me.

I knew the frustration couldn't last too much longer; the ancient, wannabe-sundial in the living room was about to chime. There was no stopping it, as I had learned, and I was about ready to burn it- along with the rest of my mother's house and all the memories that came with it- to the ground.

"If I never hear that old piece of shit again, it'll be too soon." I stormed out of the bathroom, not caring if the door slammed into the wall; the hole would vanish by morning anyways, with how repetitive my days had become. On my way to the front of the house, I glared at my mother's grandfather clock. 10:59AM.

"Commence the chimes," I proclaimed, bowing like an angry butler. "Oh! I almost forgot! How dare I!"

I turned towards the front door, placing one hand behind my back, the other holding an imaginary towel against the front of my torso. The clock groaned as it rang out in a dreary alarm, and I pointed my nose towards the ceiling as I galloped. It was time for someone to show, like a perfect little teatime.

"Not fucking interested, my good sir!" I yelled while throwing the front door open. But to my surprise, there wasn't anyone there. For the first time in five days, a stupid little face- adorned by a shiny new badge and radiating a superiority complex- wasn't waiting on my doorstep.

"You're joking," I muttered under my breath, dropping my hands to my sides. I stepped out onto the patio and peered around at the surprisingly empty street. "They really gave up on me that soon?"

"Who's joking?" A familiar head popped up above the bushes- the same unkempt blonde hair bouncing like yellow springs that I had seen a few days prior. I jumped in response, knocking over a flowerpot in the process, and landed flat on my rear end. *God*, I thought as the shattered pieces poked into my skin. *I just moved this yesterday.*

"What the fuck, man?"

"Sorry, I just dropped something. I promise I wasn't lurking in your bushes or nothin'." He dusted off his pants, avoiding eye contact all the while, before proudly placing his police badge back onto his chest. "Didn't mean to scare you like that."

He came closer and reached out a hand.

"I'm Matthew, by the way."

"I know."

He helped me up, which was the first respectable thing that any of the fuckers had done all week. One would think that I would have been prepared for this conversation at that point- considering I knew every word the heifer was about to say- but nothing, and I mean nothing, can prepare a person to hear a man question something about a woman for the billionth time. Ask my ex-boyfriend.

"I came here because-"

"You came here because you want to sell me some bullshit about how I have been couped up in this house for too long," I interjected. "You'll say that you're only here out of concern, to be a friend, to offer a *lovely* helping hand. Then, after the whole charade, you'll offer to buy me a warm meal, to which I'll agree because my love for Diet Coke on a hungover stomach outweighs my suicidal ideation, and we'll trek on over to the Denny's on Fifth Street. You'll corner me in the booth, discretely hand me the crisis hotline number, and rob me of dignity I had left."

He stared at me, his eyes blinking faster than my heartrate. I withdrew my hand that was still clasped in his own, and Matthew looked over his shoulder with a gulp. Of course, there was nobody there to explain how I knew everything. The answer was too simple- I just knew.

"Well," Matthew began in a cracked voice, "Would you prefer Waffle House?"

"Goodbye, Matthew." I stepped back into the house, the only difference that day being the hesitation to close the door.

Breakup Party

"Black cherry," I cried into my phone. "Black cherry is the best seltzer flavor."

Streetlights buzzed overhead as I sped down I-55. Gripping the steering wheel so tightly that my knuckles were white, I hardly noticed anything but the tingling sensation in my hands. Tears streamed down my face at an astonishing rate, to which I occasionally used a clenched fist to brush them away; my eyes blurring from the strain. I could somewhat make out the speed limit signs- some being engraved in my mind from the frequent trips down the interstate- but it didn't matter anyway. Deep down, I secretly hoped that my car hitting a puddle at such a high speed would land me in a ditch. At least *then* he would be obligated to come to my rescue.

It had started raining not too long before I began my hour-long drive home, but I wasn't going to let that stop me. I was going to make it back. To him. To home.

"Okay," he finally uttered with a sigh. "I'll get 'em. Turn off your location as soon as you get the chance."

And just like that, I embarked on one of the best worst nights of my life.

◇

When I walked into the house, I was greeted with the most familiar smells. His mother always had expensive candles burning in each room, no matter the time of day or occasion. Per her rules, I peeled my shoes off and habitually left them by the doorway.

Cinnamon? I asked myself. *No, she never cared for cinnamon. Apple pie. She loved that scent.*

"Wow," I exclaimed, a bit too loudly, as I turned to face him. Remnants of raindrops dripped down the lingering hair follicles he had left. The haircut was new. Probably his mother's doing- he always wanted to grow his hair out so that it could flow out of his cowboy hat. "It's the same as it was before."

And it really was. Nothing was out of place; the red chair his mother had bought at some boutique last year was still in its corner, the warm tiles in the kitchen were still clean enough to eat off of, and even the damn aloe plant they kept near the door seemed to have stayed the same length.

I assumed he still had his favorite snacks in the fridge- freshly washed grapes plucked from the vine, hard boiled eggs for a quick shot of protein in the mornings, and bottles of Dasani water that he would go through like crazy. Upstairs, the den would presumably be untouched. Our belongings were probably tucked away in some box.

Our belongings I repeated in my head.

"Hey, do you still have the stuff I got you in Florida?" I asked while cocking my head sideways. His cheeks turned crimson, and he ran a hand through his hair.

I grabbed a seltzer from the case, pressing it firmly into my hands and letting the coolness of the condensation calm my nerves while waiting for a response. I could have drunk the entire box in one setting with the way my heart was beating out of my chest. But I merely sipped on one as discretely and modestly as possible; Sam always loved how composed I could come across as. He followed suit in reaching for a seltzer before turning my direction to the staircase, nodding.

"Yeah, it's all upstairs."

"Even the blue starfish?"

Sam let out an unexpected laugh. "Yes, even the blue starfish."

Before I realized and had a chance to stop myself, I jumped for joy like a small child. He still had it all, just as I had guessed. I raced up the stairs, each footstep taking me closer to my past. I always loved reminiscing, walking down a road of altered memories, as it was the only appropriate way to visit him.

◇

The questions started after we had both gotten a few drinks deep. Sam never drank, so having two White Claws was enough to bring out his brutal honesty. I, on the other hand, was going on my fifth when I first began to look at him through a drunken gaze.

"Wanna play Twenty-One Questions?" Sam posed while reaching for the TV remote. "I'll put on some music. You can ask the first question."

I looked around the room, knowing I didn't have a choice, and searched for a question that wouldn't come. Twenty-One Questions was so much easier in middle school, when all we knew to ask was, "What's your favorite color," or, "How many people have you kissed?". So innocent, yet so risqué. Now, I had so many real questions.

Why'd you leave? Was it worth it? Do you miss me as much as I miss you? Why did you do it? Why did you do her? Am I here for you or for me? What if he finds out? I told him we were over, so it shouldn't matter. But it will. He'll think it's just another grasp for attention. Maybe if I-

"Earth to Kennedy," Sam teased, drunkenly waving a hand in front of my face. I smacked at it out of irritation.

"Sorry. Just can't think of any good ones right now."

If he had been sober, I know he would have picked up on the tone of my voice. He would have instantly asked what he did wrong, why I was so upset all of a sudden. It was too frequent of an occurrence for us for him not to. Or maybe he just didn't care at that point. But my brain will never accept that as the correct answer.

"Fine," he slurred. "I'll go first. Why are you here tonight? Don't you have that boy-toy Jordan?"

I hit my vape, allowing the smoke to slowly creep out in little O's. He knew the answer just as well as I did.

"Why do you ask?"

"Because I want to know why you're here."

"You know why I'm here."

"No, I don't."

"Yes, you do."

"Then why would I ask?"

"I don't know. Why would you?"

"I don't know."

"You invited me here."

In all of my life, I had never heard a silence so loud. The television remote still sat in his hand, the cursor looming over the unopened YouTube application. Even if music *had* been playing, the gap between our responses would have been equally as deafening.

"Have you been with anyone else?" I blurted out. "I mean, you can't exactly criticize me if you've done the same."

"No, you moron." He turned back to the television. "You wanna listen to Tyler Childers?"

That was the thing with Sam. He could always go right back to whatever tomfoolery he was doing, no matter the depth of an issue at hand. He loved to focus on anything except what really mattered, claiming he feared the emotional aspect of being human. But with me, he didn't have a choice. He knew he had to feel things.

Truth be told, I loved Tyler Childers. Our relationship initially blossomed over our love for music. I even went to one of his shows after we had broken up. Everyone stood there cheering him on, but it was all I could do to sit and watch the way he played, every beat hitting my soul in a newer, even more damaging way than before. The same drums I had sat behind, his hands on mine, teaching me the art he held so close to his heart. His voice in my ear, whispering in a voice so godlike, so soft. Afterwards, I would read him my poetry with a glimmer of hope in my eyes for the first time ever.

It hurt how familiar all of it was. The bass. The snare. The vibrations. The swirl of a drumstick in his fingertips. All of it colliding together in perfect harmony, just like us in the beginning, before I ruined everything I had ever known to be true. I almost wanted him to play "Lady May", something to prove that his longing for me still surfaced every now and again, even when the leaves fell- the colors blending together in a twister of decay. I wanted him to prove that our future wedding song still loomed in his mind. Instead, he played fucking "Beverly Hills" by Weezer, and I *still* found myself crying in the basement bathroom of the club.

I often wondered why he changed the setlist. No more Arctic Monkeys and their sexual persuasion. No more Tame Impala and their love beyond bounds. Just Nirvana and Weezer. The only two loves he had ever truly owned up to having. Moreover, I questioned why I didn't have the heart to tell anyone that he kept fucking up the chorus because he always found my eyes at that time.

My best friend Tabby spoke under her breath to me that night, complaining about losing her voice. I responded how much I wish I had lost mine; to be unable to speak to him is all I wanted. No more contact. No looming profile picture containing the most poignant hazel eyes I had ever seen. No more Siri suggestions to call "My Honey" on speaker. No more Google Maps timers to tell me how far it is to his house- 1.2 miles to be precise-, a drive I never thought I would make again.

As the LEDs flashed blue, I wondered why he never came to the hospital. As "Teen Spirit" played, I asked myself why he never visited or called, why he failed me at every single turn and opportunity I threw his way, why I sat there, a size large gown tied tightly and still falling off of my shoulders, waiting for him to apologize. But maybe it was me. Maybe it was always me. I had put myself in the psych ward, so why should I have expected him to ride in on a white horse to save me?

After the hospital, every notification, message, and side comment made in our friend group was a spew of hatred. Did I cause it? Was it the alcohol? The tattoo he dismissed without a second thought- a skeleton's hand holding a bottle with the decaying roses he left me with?

I think I'm beautiful. And strong. Much stronger than he said I was. He said I can't cope, which I coped with. He said I can't function, to which I went on functioning with. And he said I rely on him to survive, he of which I learned to survive without.

I knew he was lying about not being with anyone else. I had seen it myself at the party.

"To answer your question," I finally spoke, "I know you better than anyone else. Just like you do with me. That's why I'm really here." I clutched my hands in my lap, looking down at the carpet beneath my feet. "I'm here because I need you."

◇

"Just jump in," I laughed, waving him over as if he wasn't turned away from me. "The water's so warm."

The in-ground pool his parents owned had just been cleaned and renovated, and there I was- butt-ass naked doing backstrokes in front at *least* three security cameras. How we managed to go from serious conversing to completely stripping is beyond me, much like how the entire night is a mosaic of moments I had to glue together later on.

"Don't judge me, please. I haven't seen tits in over a month now."

"Not since mine?"

"Not since yours."

"Hmm," I rolled my eyes.

Sam turned around, his hands clasped tightly over his crotch. I laughed, splashing water towards the deck he stood on.

"You're no fun," I booed. "You get to see all of me. And it's not like I haven't seen it before."

"This is different, and you know it." He paused, looking at me with bulging eyes. "Can you just… turn around or something?"

I rolled my eyes but faced away from him, nonetheless. He had never been shameful or shy before that, and the thought of him being bashful around me made my blood run cold.

When Sam hit the water, I dived underneath to meet his gaze. He smiled, pulling me in close so he could kiss me in the depths of the chlorine. I savored the touch; he tasted like familiarity and booze… not that there was much of a difference between the two at that point.

When we emerged from the waves, I hesitated to let go of him. His response was to kiss me again and again, pressing harder with each peck as if he, too, had forgotten how addictive each other's bodies were. My breasts pushed against the warmth of his chest, his heart beating so quickly that I thought it would explode. I ran my hands through the wet tangles on his head before gripping the nape of his neck, to which he hoisted me up, positioned me just above the length of him, and pulled his head back from me to make the most lustful of eye contact.

"I want you," he grumbled.

"I'm aware of that," I giggled, glancing at our bodies tangled in one another.

"No. Not like that. Well, of course I always want you like that. But, Ken. I need you to get better. I can't have my future wife being like this."

"Being like what?" *Future wife? He still wants me?* I drew back from him, attempting to get him to let me go. He instead held tighter to my thighs.

"You know what I mean."

"Why didn't you call me?"

"What?"

"Why didn't you call me? When I was in in-patient."

"I gave you my phone number. Why didn't you call me?"

"Because I wanted you to want me."

"I *do* want you."

"No, you don't."

"Shut up and kiss me."

He pulled me back in, and I failed to withdraw. We eventually wound up in his mother's hot tub in an abnormally sized bathroom. We drank, made love, and screamed Tyler Childers lyrics for the rest of the night, with me being blissfully unaware that it would all crash again by the break of dawn.

◇

When I awoke, I found myself alone in his bedroom. My head pulsated with each heartbeat, and I squinted while glancing around the room for my clothing. Not a single thing was out of place… except for me.

"Fuck," I mumbled while rolling over to reach for my phone. "*Fuck.*"

I read the text message from Sam, ignoring the dozens of missed calls from my friends.

Getting breakfast this morning with Connie. Your clothes are in the bathroom floor. Please be gone before the guys get there. Don't want them to assume anything.

I sat there for a second, unsure of what to say. I had so many words, but I knew that none of them would truly land in his mind. So, instead of embarking on another apologetic journey, I merely sent an, "Okay." And from then on, I waited on another text that would never come.

The Countdown

8:29 PM- Three Hours, Thirty-One Minutes

Only three hours, thirty-one minutes left now. Ask me five years ago, I would have told you that I would be dead by now. Ask me six years ago, you would have learned about my destiny in Los Angles- how I would become an award-winning actress. Ask me seven years ago, I would have been a published author with Pulitzer prizes tumbling from the depths of my closet onto the floor of my eight-story mansion in New York City. But ask me now, and I will guide your gaze to the things about me of which I cannot look at myself. Wrinkles, presumably from laugh lines, shamefully carve themselves into my not-so-smooth-anymore skin. Acne of which I never struggled with before pops up like the little miniature weasels you smack with a hammer at Chuck-E-Cheese. And most of all, my breasts have begun to sag, slowly creeping away from my once ever-so-feminine core.

I wish I could tell my childhood self all of the accomplishments I have made, but they are so few and far between. She will instead be informed of how acting is something she won't be too great at. How the death of her only brother would teach her that suicide is the easy way out, leaving more pain than entrails in the household, car, or wherever else she had considered. How playing Junie B. Jones' mother in her town's run-down theater would be the closest thing to Veronica Sawyer in Broadway's *Heathers: The Musical* that she would achieve. How her ability to write is strong enough to win first place at BetaCon's state and third place at nationals, but not mighty enough to snag a job at her small town's newspaper company. How her skin, like her poetry, may be acknowledged by many but discarded by most. How she will sit in her mother's house in her junior year of college, the night before her twenty-first birthday, and reflect on her inability to pay rent, her childhood that comes back to her more and more with every bowl she smokes, her failures and losses, how she never met the goal of publishing a novel before her teenage years ran out, and how her fear of the world will forever hold her back.

9:04PM- Two Hours, Fifty-Six Minutes

I wonder if the Chuck-E-Cheese I went to as a child still stands today. If so, the workers are all new and probably much more depressed than I remember. None of them have heard my laughter, though all children emit the same sound of joy and innocence among animatronics, pizza buffets, and challenging games. Perhaps the games have been swapped, too. Instead of side-by-side basketball hoops, begging to be played by parent and child, surely there is an animated version in its place. Stacker- the game I always won because of my concentration, hyper fixation, and/or pure luck of pressing a single damn button repetitively- is most likely the PacMan of our generation; it was great while it lasted but is merely nostalgia to us and yawn-inducing to today's children. Just a few years ago, I was perplexed by the addition of a Deal or No Deal game being added to the place. Where had the hands-on stuff gone? The physical release of endorphins and serotonin through sweat and shouting at friends? The balls that were pitched at wooden birds behind a cage? Had they grown up too? Why had they flown away while I was still in the nest?

Are the prizes the same? Surely not. Mini Tootsie Pops, shitty rubber band bracelets/rings, color changing pencils, basic rubber ducks, stickers that weren't sticky, and Slinkys are all outdated- much like myself, I fear. I wish I could tell my younger self that she would win one of the cool prizes someday, or that her mother would eventually be able to afford enough tickets to even stand a chance of doing so. But the fact of the matter is this- her blue Airheads and little green yo-yo will bring the same joy that an overpriced soccer ball or stuffed Chuck would. Just like her mother used to say, "You can get so many small things, or you can get one big one. Wouldn't you rather have more?" To which her yearning for everything at once would solidify.

9:38PM- Two Hours, Twenty-Two Minutes

9:47PM- Two Hours, Thirteen Minutes

Meaningless. It's all so… meaningless. Life. Death. Birthdays. Celebrations. Stupid pizza buffets. All of it. What reason is there to keep going when all we do is die in the end? Will people still love me when I'm nothing new?

10:00PM- Two Hours

Just recently, a memory popped up on my Facebook feed from when I was maybe fourteen years old. I spoke in depth of how much I despised people who smoked marijuana, used tobacco products of any kind, binge drank alcohol, or did practically anything that was mind-altering. Have I always been this hypocritical? I can't recall.

10:10PM- One Hour, Fifty Minutes

Does anyone *really* have their shit together in their twenties? Or are we all pretending that we aren't grieving the deaths of our childhoods?

10:22PM- One Hour, Forty-Eight Minutes

Now that I think about it, growing up in the Bible Belt sure made for an interesting youth, what with the constant reminder of burning in hell for eternity masked by melodic church bells every hour. And one would think that these bells would be loudest in the summertime- considering Tennessee heat and humidity is pretty close to what I imagine hell would feel like- but they always resonated more in early fall, just before going back to elementary classes. These classes, like everything else from my childhood, can be recalled so easily. But they can never be relived. Rather, the memories can only be found in the circuitry of my brain- hidden from the world and recalled slightly differently each time.

Maybe it's because the ice cream truck was coming around less and less, and the typical tune we so desperately longed to hear was replaced by Christian chimes. Or perhaps it's due to the bells being in the background of the summer's final church supper, youth group activity, sleepover/lock-in, and bicycle ride. Regardless, the burgundy and burnt orange leaves twirled in spirals on their way to the ground as the bells gave them music to glide to, leaving the only ice cream truck in town to fade into the background.

I believe most everyone has that one sweet treat from childhood that they wish they could taste for the first time again, whether that be a SpongeBob popsicle off the ice cream truck or a classic bag of orange peanuts from a random Dollar General. For me, it was hands down vanilla Moon Pies. Not just any vanilla Moon Pie, though. They had to come from my Grandma's house on a Wednesday afternoon, just after church supper ended and the 7PM bells were going off. Dad also had to be there, mowing her lawn as she stuffed a Walmart bag full of goodies that I most certainly was not supposed to have. We would play card games together, giggling and gossiping about my dad working himself to death as we women (though I was only seven or eight years old at the time) got to enjoy the "finer" things in life. Then, almost too quickly, there they were again. The bells, signaling that it was time to go home.

    I would do anything again to taste those Moon Pies and hear those bells in the same way again. When my grandma passed, I stopped hearing the bells for a while, and if I did hear them, they were quieter and lower in pitch. Like when a radio station fades out slowly amidst a long, rainy drive- when the pellets of icy precipitation smack the windshield so loudly that you don't even recognize that the music is growing hazy and filling with static. And yet, the further you drive away from common ground, the less you realize your sense of self is drifting away faster than the clouds.

    The worst of it all is that you often drive at the same speed as the storm- 60 miles an hour or so-, meaning that you cannot outrun it; you will continue forward, searching for a destination that may or may not come. But finally, by some miracle or determination, the rain will cease. The sun will come back out. You'll change the station, and maybe you'll even sing along to an old tune. The advertisements will seem lighter in tone, allowing you to fully grasp what they are selling and causing you to consider buying whatever it is.

And you'll remember everything- the way sweat dripped from your brows in the dying heat the night before school started back, the smell of cheap cologne that your siblings wore when they were young, the taste of vegetable soup and cornbread made fresh in the church kitchen, the cooling sensation of your pillowcase and how the temperature made every muscle sink further into the mattress, and the pungent smell of craft supplies and crayons that melted on the Sunday school bus. You'll recall every room, hallway, piece of furniture, and decoration that the church held in its interior- the winding paths that felt like jungles and vines that you would swing through in your imagination. And most of all, you'll remember the taste of your favorite treat and how, even after more than a decade, you'll never want anything more than to taste it for the first time again.

10:46PM- One Hour, Fourteen Minutes

When I awake in the morning, I wonder if anything will feel different. Of course, physically nothing will change; the scar from my birth control implant will remain, the pale skin where a firework gave me a third-degree burn on my seven-year-old hand will still be apparent to all that grasp it, what my ex-boyfriend called tiger stripes will still extend from my lower back onto my hips and around my breasts, and my eyes will still be sunken in from lack of iron. My hair will still be brittle from the many hair dyes that made their way onto my follicles amidst one too many mental breakdowns. I will still have a mole on my chin, freckles across my nose that are too stubborn for even the whitest foundation, and coffee stains imprinted on my teeth. My nose will still curve upwards at the end in "Cindy Lou Who fashion", as the middle school boys used to call it, and my ears will remain elf shaped and flat at the top. Right?

10:58PM- One Hour, Two Minutes

Successful people are like flowers, I tell myself. *Each one blooms at a different rate, in differing environments and climates. Perhaps I merely slept through my season.*

11:01PM- Fifty-Nine Minutes

In beginning to plan my birthday, I realized that I can see it all now- the party lights fading from red, to blue, to green and back again while the room sits mostly empty. There will be hundreds of unused Solo cups just sitting on the counter, and the mixed drink- whatever Jungle Juice I come up with an hour prior- will leak out of the tap, hitting the ground in a rhythmic trickle. Just enough people will show for it to be embarrassing, but not humiliating. The theme will be liquor, with my outfit being an orange cocktail dress adorned by a red, LED cowboy hat. Fireball, I'll tell everyone. My best friend will wear a peach-colored hoodie but forget to buy a plastic crown, despite my relentless daily reminders that will have plagued him for over a week. I'll tell him that he can be a virgin Crown Royal Peach drink, even when he is the only one to show up remotely dressed for the theme.

I will have made 140-something Jell-O shots, flavored with red, blue, and pink Starburst packets. They'll be a little too strong, and someone will comment about it and say, "Jesus, Ken. How much vodka did you put in these? They taste like shit." The answer will be that I doubled the amount that the recipe called for because I thought everyone would enjoy themselves better. That it made it feel more 21-ish. That I feel the *need* to be obliterated. That I just got out of detox, and they know that. That I feel like people must be drunk to stand being around me for more than five minutes.

11:32PM- Forty-Three Minutes

Tomorrow, somewhere around 11:30, I bet I'll start to realize that the hundred people that promised to come were only saying that to appease my constant chatter. I'll start to fantasize about turning twenty-two, praying that it'll go just a little easier on me.

Taylor Swift's *Red* album will be on repeat the entire night, the lyrics of "All Too Well" creeping in and out of the bathroom where I lay.

He watched me watch the front door all night...
willin' you to come...
and he said, "It's supposed to be fun...
turning twenty-one..."

When I'm drunk enough, I'll eventually say, "Fuck it," and go out on the town to track down other parties. I'll stumble into the home of one of my ex-best friends, to which thirty or so people will all look at me in a disappointed gaze. I won't be able to tell (or I will be too inebriated to care) if they simply hate seeing me there or if they just hate me in general. I'll offer up what's left of the Jell-O shots. I think there'll be around 120 left, considering they were such a hit. It'll be my bittersweet apology.

11:40PM- Twenty Minutes

I'll probably bump into my most recent ex-boyfriend if I'm lucky enough to see him curled up with a new girl. But it won't be a *new* girl. It'll be someone who used to be my friend. Connie. She'll be wrapped in his arms, her curls bouncing to the beat their radiant laughter. Her freckles will glow in the apartment lights, and her oversized sweatshirt will be tightened around her hips where his hands snake around them.

    Connie will make eye-contact with me, threatening me to keep silent and mind my own. I'll want to tell her that his hands will move up slowly, further and further until they nearly choke her out. That he'll say he's just joking, even when the callouses on his palms feel like they'll make direct contact with her blood vessels. That she'll wake up black in blue from his "teases". That she'll grow to forgive him and allow him to do it all again, starting right back with his hands on her hips. That he will always be home to her. That her home is, and always has been, so broken.

    But she will already know all of that. She will have already known it all for a while.

    I'll most likely find out later that he and his ex, beautiful Jess, made-out with one another at the Halloween party just weeks prior, when he and I were still together and planning a wedding and naming our future children. That they cried together while talking about their pasts. That my unsuccessful suicide attempt scared him back into her arms. That my own downfall was the reason for reaching rock bottom. That, even though she sat and waited all night with me as the nurses flew past to sign me up for detox and in-patient, she was keeping that secret from me the entire time. *If* I ever own up to my issues and go into detox, that is.

11:46PM- Fourteen Minutes

I wonder if he'll tell me that it was all my fault to begin with. That, because I was so emotional about the things that mattered to me, he had to seek refuge somewhere else. *Once I saved you from suicide the first time,* he'll say, *I thought the darkness was gone for good. But it came back. And I just can't handle that shit. It's too much.* And I'll agree, bowing my head in shame.

11:47PM- Thirteen Minutes

Has it always been my fault? Have I always suffered in having a hair-trigger, or am I just too sensitive? Jess might say it's Borderline Personality Disorder. I may say I just care a little too much.

11:49PM- Eleven Minutes

I want to call him. Even if he just puts his hands on my body for five stupid minutes. It'd be enough.

12:00AM- Zero Minutes

A shitty new chapter has begun. Here's to motherfucking twenty-one.

Made in the USA
Columbia, SC
16 May 2023